My Garden in Spring

Katie Smythe

New York

It is spring.

This is my garden.

I put soil in my garden.
Flowers grow in soil.

It rains in the spring.

Rain is good for my garden.

I water my flowers
when it does not rain.
Water helps my flowers grow.

Tulips bloom in the spring.

Tulips grow from bulbs.

I pick the tulips.

Daffodils also bloom
in the spring.
Daffodils grow from seeds.

I see weeds in my garden.

I pull them out of the soil.

Weeds are bad for my garden.

Sometimes I see frogs
in my garden.
Frogs eat bugs
that hurt my garden.
Frogs are good for my garden.

Worms are also
good for my garden.
They dig through the soil
and keep it soft.

I like to take care of my garden.
What would you like to grow
in your garden?

Words to Know

daffodil

frog

garden

soil

tulip

worm